## How the book is laid out

*Example – Wild Thyme*

**Current s...**
**evidence...**

**FLOWERI...**

**HEIGHT ...**

**WHEN TO...**

**DESCRIPT...**
**stems, fru...**

**HABITAT ...**
**together with good areas/sites to see
the species.**

**HOW TO USE** *Historic, culinary and medicinal
uses are mentioned, together with the
folklore associated with each species.
Ideas for uses, with some recipes, are
also provided.*

**DID YOU KNOW?** *Extra facts about
the species*

## Foraging for wild plants (flowers, leaves, berries and nuts)
When looking for wild food please follow the country code. It is illegal to uproot any plant without the permission of the landowner. **Care should be taken in identifying wild plants – if in doubt of the identity of *any* plant, do not pick with a meal in mind.**

## Foraging for fungi
**Do not collect fungi to eat unless you are quite sure that you have identified them correctly**, and please adhere to the *Wild mushroom pickers' Code of Conduct* (reproduced on p. 73).

**Similar species** – it is important that all the features check out when identifying a fungus, as some very poisonous fungi can, at first glance, look almost the same as an edible species, such as the examples below. **Remember, never eat a fungus unless you are quite sure that you have identified it correctly.**

**Wood
Mushroom**
*Agaricus silvicola*
(edible)

**Deathcap**
*Amanita phalliodes*
(deadly
poisonous)

**Check underneath the cap** – most fungi have gills attached to the underside of the cap, but some, mainly boletes (see Cep p. 59) and some bracket fungi (pp. 51 and 53), have tubes which look like spongy pores. The colour of the gills/pores can change once the spores have dropped, or they may bruise a different colour, or exude

**How are the gills attached to the stem?** – The way the gills are attached to the stem can differ, and can be an important identification feature.

Free of stem
(described as **free**
in most guides)

Narrowly attached to stem
(described as **adnexed**
in most guides)

Broadly attached to stem
(described as **adnate**
in most guides)

Running down onto stem
(described as **decurrent**
in most guides)

# Gorse

*Ulex europaea*

**FLOWERING TIME** Mainly January-June, but appear all year

**HEIGHT** 2–3m

**WHEN TO FORAGE** Pick flowers when they are out fully

**DESCRIPTION** Also known as 'Furze' or 'Whin', Gorse is a fast-growing and abundant evergreen shrub with sharp blue-green spines for leaves and vibrant golden-yellow flowers. It is a member of the pea family with distinctively shaped flowers, like those of a garden pea or bean. The main flowering season is spring and the flowers are at their best between April and June, but can be found in any month of the year. It is often planted as a hedge or windbreak for livestock, and in the past was grown near dwellings so that washing could be laid out to dry on the thorny branches without fear of it blowing away. On hot summer days when the seeds are ripe, the hairy pods burst explosively and the seeds are flung far and wide. Its cousin, **Dwarf Gorse *Ulex minor***, only reaches 20cm in height. Unlike Gorse, the flowers are not scented. Several birds make use of Gorse as perching posts and nesting sites, including linnets, stonechats and the rare Dartford warbler.

**HABITAT** You will find swathes of Gorse on areas of heathland (especially in Berkshire, where you will also find Dwarf Gorse) and in rough, grassy areas such as commons and on the tops of the Chilterns and Cotswolds.

**HOW TO USE** Gorse flowers are edible and have a 'coconutty' scent and flavour. The buds can be used to make tea and the flowers can be added to salads and to produce a wine that tastes both nutty and flowery and goes well with fish. When picked in January the flowers can add a welcome sprinkle of colour to your winter greens. Traditionally, Gorse had a multitude of uses as fuel to burn in bread ovens, cattle feed, as chimney brushes and as a source of colour for Easter eggs. Use thick gardening gloves to pick Gorse flowers so that you aren't scratched by the prickly stems.

## DID YOU KNOW?

There is an old country saying known throughout Britain that goes 'When Gorse is out of blossom, kissing is out of fashion'.

4

# Dandelion
*Taraxacum officinale*

**FLOWERING TIME** February–November, especially April and May

**HEIGHT** 5–40cm

**WHEN TO FORAGE** Leaves can be collected almost any time of year.

**DESCRIPTION** Dandelions are so common and well-known that everyone will be able to identify them. Their wide open, sun-like flowers are in bloom in almost all seasons, but especially in spring when little else is on show. They vary greatly in size from short, down-trodden plants in lawns to leggy specimens where they are competing for light among other vegetation. The resemblance of the sharp, pointed leaves to the teeth of a lion give the flower its common name. These form a flat rosette at the base of the plant. Several long-stalked flowerheads may grow from the base. When the flowers has gone over, the seedheads or 'pappuses' of the dandelion make a clock, which generations of children have used to 'tell the time'.

**HABITAT** The Dandelion is one of the most common weeds in Britain and is widely found throughout the three counties in bare and grassy places including gardens, roadside verges, fields and waste ground.

**HOW TO USE** Dandelions have many uses in the kitchen. The edible leaves, which have a high content of vitamins A and C, can be used in salads, soups and sandwiches (the latter, with a dash of Worcester sauce), or cooked with butter. Young, tender leaves are best. The flowers can be made into wines, beers and a lemonade or 'fizz'. Traditionally dandelions were gathered on St George's Day (23 April) to make wine. Wild Food writer, Roger Phillips, describes how Dandelion beer was the favourite countryside tipple of workers in iron foundries and potteries because it was so refreshing and settled stomach upsets. In times of rationing, particularly during the Second World War, the roots were roasted and ground into a coffee substitute. For a wholesome broth, Dandelion soup made with potatoes, onions and chicken stock is worth trying. For something spicy, try Dandelion flower bhajis.

## DID YOU KNOW?

Also known as 'Wet-the-bed' and 'Tiddlebeds', Dandelion has been recognised as a diuretic for centuries and used by herbalists such as Nicholas Culpeper to purify the blood.

# Common Nettle

*Urtica dioica*

**FLOWERING TIME** May–October

**HEIGHT** Up to 152cm

**WHEN TO FORAGE** Pick leaves (using gloves), before the beginning of June

**DESCRIPTION** This perennial herb with powerful stinging hairs is also known as 'Stinging nettle', 'Devil's plaything' and 'Hokey-pokey'. The mechanism that causes the sting are the tips of the hairs on the leaves being broken off and releasing an acid which causes an itchy rash. Creeping, rooting stems produce upright, leafy stems with heart-shaped, toothed leaves. On female plants the flower clusters hang down while on male plants the clusters stick out. It is best to pick young leaves and plant tips because by high summer the leaves become tough and bitter. (Caution: remember to wear a pair of gardening gloves.)

**HABITAT** Common Nettles grow in abundance in large patches in fertile soil found in many different habitats, from hedgebanks, woodland glades and river valleys, to gardens, churchyards and waste ground near buildings. In *Flora Britannica*, Richard Mabey notes that it gives its name to half a dozen villages in Britain, including Nettlebed near Henley-on-Thames, in Oxfordshire.

**HOW TO USE** Nettles have been used as a food, medicine and cloth since prehistoric times and were readily used by the Romans and Celts. The early herbals are full of nettle remedies for nose bleeds, cancers and paralysed limbs and as an antidote for poison. Nettles contain iron, formic acid, silicic acid and histamine and are still recognised for their ability to improve the circulation and lower blood pressure and blood sugar levels. Modern cooks tend to pick young and tender Nettles to use as a steamed fresh vegetable, wilted down with butter and nutmeg or boiled in water with a pinch of salt. Nettles can also be puréed in soups or served with a poached egg. Dried leaves can be made into a dark-green tea by infusing the leaves for just five minutes then straining the liquid into a cup. Nettle wine, a medium sweet white wine can be made with yeast, lemons, water, sugar and root ginger.

## DID YOU KNOW?

The Common Nettle is the larval foodplant of many of our beautiful butterflies including the Peacock, Small Tortoiseshell, Comma and Red Admiral.

# Ramsons or Wild Garlic

*Allium ursinum*

**FLOWERING TIME** April–June

**HEIGHT** Up to 50cm

**WHEN TO FORAGE** Pick flowers when they are out fully

**DESCRIPTION** One of the highlights of spring is letting your nose lead you into a glade filled with Wild Garlic, also known as Ramsons, Broad-leaved Garlic, 'stink bombs' and 'Londoner's lilies'. The flowers are beautiful, with six bright white petals, held on long triangular stalks and forming loose umbels of starry blossoms in late spring, before the canopy of broad-leaved trees casts its shade. The leaves grow from the root on square separate stems. They are broadly elliptical and spear-shaped, tapering to a point. It is the leaves that are used in cooking and when broken smell strongly of garlic. **(Caution: Do not mistake them with the similar-looking, poisonous leaves of Lily-of-the-Valley *Convallaria majalis* which have no scent when torn, and is rare in our area. Wild Garlic leaves are also a brighter green.)**

**HABITAT** This bulbous plant is widespread and locally plentiful in the damper parts of ancient woodlands and shady hedgebanks, forming dense and sometimes extensive colonies. The Wychwood area, the Oxfordshire Cotswolds and some Chilterns woodlands are particularly good places to experience the all-pervasive smell of a Wild Garlic wood.

**HOW TO USE** Seventeenth-century herbalist, Nicholas Culpeper, was most effusive about the powerful properties of Wild Garlic, including their use for the relief of asthma. Wild Garlic is also good for wildlife too, it is used by plenty of pollinating insects including hoverflies, butterflies and longhorn beetles. To make use of Wild Garlic in your kitchen chop the leaves crosswise and add to salads, soups, stews and pasta sauces. When finely chopped and mixed with lemon juice, olive oil and grated parmesan, the leaves also make a tasty Wild Garlic pesto. Also try the leaves chopped into sour cream, made into a Wild Garlic butter, or laid onto a tomato salad. When cooked the flavour of Wild Garlic tends to fade so large quantities will be needed for a stronger flavour.

### DID YOU KNOW?

Cultivated garlic was used as an antiseptic during the Second World War. Juice from the bulbs was applied to swabs of sphagnum moss.

# Common Sorrel

*Rumex acetosa*

**FLOWERING TIME** May–August

**HEIGHT** 10–20cm

**WHEN TO FORAGE** From February

**DESCRIPTION** A sturdy, upright perennial herb with roots that run deep into the ground. It has branched spikes of tiny flowers and arrow-shaped leaves. The upper leaves are almost stalkless and clasp the stem. As the leaves come through in early spring, it can be picked at any time of year when other green flavourings and vegetables are scarce. In late summer, Common Sorrel adds a vivid dash of red to the grassy places where it grows, as the leaves, stems, flowers and fruits turn a deep crimson.

**HABITAT** Common Sorrel, otherwise known as 'spinach dock' or 'narrow-leaved dock', is very common in fields and hedgerows, including roadside banks and in open places in woods. You only have to nibble the edge of a leaf and taste its lemony tang to recognise it instantly.

**HOW TO USE** The chopped-up leaves of Common Sorrel are noticeably sharp in taste, hence the plant's other names of 'sour docks' 'sour ducks' and 'vinegar leaves'. They were traditionally used for flavouring in much the same way as lemons are used today. In Tudor times, Sorrel was a highly prized English vegetable, gracing the table of Henry VIII and used as a green sauce with cold meats, until it was replaced by French Sorrel. Common Sorrel is used extensively in French cuisine to provide a sharp contrast to heavy potato and bean dishes as well as rich, fatty foods like pork and oily fish. It is also used in omelettes, salads and soups. To make a tasty Common Sorrel autumn soup, add a handful of washed leaves to fried, chopped onion and a diced potato and cook for three minutes. Blend together with 500ml of stock and serve with homemade bread.

**DID YOU KNOW?**

All of the early herbalists were full of praise for the cooling properties of Common Sorrel. Today, infusions of sorrel are used to aid throat and mouth ulcers.

# Wood-sorrel

*Oxalis acetosella*

**FLOWERING TIME** April–May

**HEIGHT** 5–15cm

**WHEN TO FORAGE** Spring

**DESCRIPTION** This delicate woodland plant has a variety of old names including 'Alleluia', 'Cuckoo's bread and cheese' and 'Granny's sour grass'. The bright green leaves are folded to begin with, in the shape of a little hat, then open flat as three heart shapes with their points joined at the stem. These leaflets fold down at night giving rise to other popular names such as 'sleeping beauty' and 'sleeping clover'. Single lilac-veined white flowers usually appear between Easter and Whitsun (the week of the second May Bank holiday). Abundant nectar attracts bees and beetles. The generic scientific name of *Oxalis* refers to the sharp, acid taste of the leaves, which contain calcium oxalate.

**HABITAT** Wood-sorrel is one of the characteristic early spring-flowering plants of the woodland floor, along with Wood Anemone, Bluebell and Wild Garlic (see p. 9). It is common and widespread in ancient, broad-leaved woodlands and hedge banks often growing in clumps in shady and moist areas.

**HOW TO USE** As early as the 14th-century the leaves of Wood-sorrel were used to add flavour to salads and green sauces, and were cultivated in gardens. As a flavouring Wood-sorrel provides a lemony/vinegary taste to whatever its added to. Traditionally it was a popular compliment to fish and makes a great stuffing for fresh fish cooked on a campfire. It can be used as a green vegetable mainly in salads, or, as the leaves grow older, they can be steamed or added to soups and sauces. Boiled with sugar then allowed to cool, it also makes a sweet sorrel tea that tastes similar to lemonade. **However, it should only be used for flavouring in small quantities because it contains oxalic acid and is slightly toxic if taken in large amounts.**

**DID YOU KNOW?**

With its shamrock-shaped leaves, this plant is widely considered to have been used by St Patrick to demonstrate the Trinity to the ancient Irish.

# Wild Strawberry
*Fragaria vesca*

**FLOWERING TIME** April–July

**HEIGHT** 5–30cm

**WHEN TO FORAGE** Late June–September

**DESCRIPTION** The Wild Strawberry is a low-growing plant that uses hairy runners at intervals to form new plants. The leaves have long stalks and three leaflets that are bright green on top and pale below. Delicate white, five-petalled flowers appear from April and the small drooping berries with visible seeds ripen to a bright red in summer. The fruits can be difficult to find since they are usually hidden from view beneath the leaves. The search for these edible jewels is what makes finding Wild Strawberries such fun. Since the delicate fruits are bruised very easily, in Sweden the fruits are threaded individually onto long grass stems.

**HABITAT** Wild Strawberries are widespread in open woods, scrub, grassy banks and grassland throughout the three counties, especially on the chalky soil of the Chilterns and the dry grassland and gravels at Greenham Common in Berks.

**HOW TO USE** Strawberries have been used cosmetically for removing stains from teeth and whitening sunburnt skin. Historically, the leaves and fruit were used medicinally in fevers, dysentery and thought to be a cure for gout. Today, there is no better way to savour the flavour of a Wild Strawberry than eating it straight from the plant, or with a squeeze of orange juice, a sprinkling of sugar and lightly whipped cream. If you are lucky enough to find a sizeable crop, you could make strawberry fritters in a frothy batter, or add to a fresh fruit salad. They can also be used as the main ingredient in ice cream, cocktails, jams, tarts and vinaigrettes. Complimentary pairings include cream, vanilla, coconut, caramel, aged cheeses, blue cheese and herbs such as basil and mint. The taste is more delicate than the cultivated larger varieties available in greengrocers and supermarkets.

**DID YOU KNOW?**

The name strawberry arose because the running stems of the plants are strewed or 'strawed' over the ground, not because they are often bedded on straw to keep them clean.

# Elder

*Sambucus nigra*

**FLOWERING TIME** June

**HEIGHT** Up to 10m

**WHEN TO FORAGE** Flowerheads in June, berries from August–October

**DESCRIPTION** A vigorous and fast-growing bushy shrub with stalked, toothed leaves that are opposite, consisting of five to seven leaflets which do not smell very pleasant. In June, frothy, creamy-white flowers form a flat-topped head with a heavy, sweet scent. In autumn, the berries ripen to a deep purple-black and droop upside down in clusters. **(Caution: do not mistake for the poisonous Dwarf Elder *Sambucus ebulus*, which is no higher than 1.5m, and has non-drooping black berries.)** Many garden and woodland birds feast on Elderberries, from Robins and Blackbirds, to Blue Tits, Song Thrushes and Dunnocks. Every autumn they unwittingly help to propagate the plant throughout the countryside.

**HABITAT** Elder is commonly occurring in hedgerows, woods, chalk downs, waste ground and cultivated land across the three counties. It flourishes wherever the nitrogen content of the soil is high: near abandoned buildings, in churchyards and around rabbit warrens and badger setts.

**HOW TO USE** In the past all parts of the Elder tree were used, from the bark and the buds to the flowers and the berries. The wood was commonly made into skewers for butchers, tops for fishing rods and needles for weaving nets. Dyes were also obtained from different parts of the tree: the Romans used the juice from berries to create a hair dye, black was made from the bark, green from the leaves and blue from the flowers. Today, the fruits and flowers are good for wines and a variety of drinks including the deliciously fragrant Elderflower cordial and a 'champagne'. Elderflower fritters, using the whole head of the flower, sprinkled with sugar and served with ice cream are a personal favourite. The berries can be combined with apples or other wild berries to make preserves, jellies and pies. Elderberry cordial has long been used as a remedy for colds and coughs.

**DID YOU KNOW?**

According to folklore, you should always tell the tree what you are doing and why, if you need to pick its flowers or berries.

18

# Marjoram

*Origanum vulgare*

**FLOWERING TIME** July–October

**HEIGHT** Up to 1m

**WHEN TO FORAGE** Pick sprigs when the plant is in full flower

**DESCRIPTION** Marjoram is a perennial plant, also known as Oregano. It has slender stems that branch at the top and oval leaves that have short stalks and grow in opposite pairs. The small, lilac-coloured flowers grow in loose heads and have purplish bracts. They appear throughout summer. The entire plant is downy and aromatic, especially when a leaf or two is crushed. Brushing through swathes of fragrant Marjoram is a true highlight of a midsummer walk.

**HABITAT** Marjoram grows in dry grassland, hedgebanks, scrub and sunny hillsides, particularly the chalky slopes of the Chilterns and the Downs. Head to the limestone country of west Oxfordshire and the coral limestone ridge running from Faringdon in the west towards Oakley in Bucks.

**HOW TO USE** The medicinal use of Marjoram dates back to ancient times. The Greeks used it for healing wounds, and early herbalists made tea infusions for coughs, stomach upsets and earache. It was also used as a strewing herb, as a flavouring for ale and tea, and as a red and purple dye. In the past the plant was also popular for making herbal sachets and sweet-smelling powders. As a delicious, fragrant herb in use today, it is most often added as a garnish to salads and as a flavouring to meat in stews, casseroles, shepherd's pies and spaghetti sauces. Always add the chopped herb towards the end of cooking or the delicate flavour will be lost. It becomes sweeter when it is dried and retains its fragrance and can then be used in a wider range of dishes such as herb scones, and for flavouring sugar in cake baking.

### DID YOU KNOW?

A sure sign that you have found Marjoram is the sight of the Small Purple and Gold *Pyrausta aurata*, a tiny day-flying moth, often seen in numbers on the flowers or fluttering around the leaves.

# Wild Thyme
*Thymus polytrichus*

**FLOWERING TIME** May–August

**HEIGHT** 5–10cm

**WHEN TO FORAGE** Best picked when in full flower

**DESCRIPTION** This low-growing wiry plant with pretty pink-purple flowers has a delicious scent and has inspired writers and poets through the ages, including William Shakespeare in *A Midsummer Night's Dream* where Oberon, king of the fairies observes, 'I know a bank whereupon the wild thyme blows/Where oxlips and the nodding violet grows...'. It often grows in extensive mats and when trodden underfoot the tiny, oval leaves release the volatile oil, thymol. The flowers are much-loved by bees and other pollinating insects. In the Middle Ages ladies embroidered symbolic favours for their suitors showing a bee alighting a sprig of Wild Thyme. **Large Thyme *Thymus pulegioides*** is also found in our three counties but is generally taller to 25cm and has longer flowerheads.

**HABITAT** Wild Thyme is most abundant in grassy places with dry, chalky soil in sunny positions, particularly south-facing slopes in the Chilterns.

**HOW TO USE** Together with mint and sage, thyme is one of Britain's best-known and most used culinary herbs. When used in cooking Wild Thyme is only mildly aromatic and less pungent than garden varieties, so you will need to use large sprigs. It is a lovely flavouring for any savoury dish including vegetables, stuffings and especially roasting meat. Finely chopped, it also compliments omelette and mushroom dishes. Tea can be made using the leaves which is good for coughs and colds. In the Scottish Highlands tea made from thyme was once believed to prevent nightmares. Thyme oil, made from the leaves and flowering tops, is a recognised anti-spasmodic still used in medicines for whooping cough and bronchitis. Wild Thyme can be dried and stored very well and adds the flavour of summer to a winter meal.

**DID YOU KNOW?**

In Britain, Wild Thyme was long regarded as the favourite flower of the fairies, who loved its sweet and delicate fragrance.

# Wild Basil

*Clinopodium vulgare*

**FLOWERING TIME** July–September

**HEIGHT** Up to 45cm

**WHEN TO FORAGE** Late summer

**DESCRIPTION** Wild Basil, also known as 'hedge basil' or 'wood basil', neither looks or smells like its culinary cousin. It is a cheery, if somewhat straggly and rather untidy looking plant, with numerous usually unbranched stems forming clumps. The hairy leaves are oval and slightly toothed. It has pinkish-purple flowers in whorls up the stem and is in flower from midsummer to early autumn. Each flower is two-lipped. A downy dome-shaped cluster on top gives the plant its other name of 'cushion calamint'.

**HABITAT** Wild Basil grows in dry hedge-banks, woodland margins, scrub, quarries and waste ground as well as on chalk and limestone grassland. You can find it mainly in the Chilterns, Lambourn Downs, Oxfordshire Cotswolds, and along the corallian limestone ridge that runs from Faringdon in the west to Beckley just north of Oxford.

**HOW TO USE** In the Middle Ages, the aromatic Wild Basil was carried in posies by judges and other officials to protect themselves from unpleasant smells, which they believed harboured diseases. Before proper sanitation was introduced, it was also strewn on the floor with rushes. In the 17th-century the herbalist Culpeper recommended the calamint group of plants as a cure for afflictions of the brain, as well as a cure for jaundice, leprosy, convulsions and cramp. In the kitchen today, Wild Basil can be used fresh in salads and it works especially well with tomatoes. Since its flavour is mild you will need large quantities of chopped leaves for a noticeable flavour. A sweet and aromatic herb tea can also be made from the fresh leaves. Dried leaves can be added to soups and stews.

## DID YOU KNOW?

In ancient times the plant was said to repel serpents, particularly the legendary basilisk which had the power to kill all life by its stare.

24

# Water Mint
## *Mentha aquatica*

**FLOWERING TIME** July–September

**HEIGHT** Up to 60cm

**WHEN TO FORAGE** Just as the plant is coming into flower

**DESCRIPTION** This upright perennial plant has reddish stems with light green oval leaves, stalked and hairy on both sides. The flower spikes have pinkish-purple flowers arranged in a series of whorled clusters up the stem and are topped with a final rounded head. Water Mint can grow in extensive clumps by waterside habitats and also damp grassland and ditches. The less common **Corn Mint** ***Mentha arvensis*** is similar but does not have the terminal head of flowers.

**HABITAT** Water Mint is the most common of all mint species and grows in almost any watery or damp place, including fens, marshes, ditches, ponds and riverbanks throughout the three counties.

**HOW TO USE** Mint is an ancient herb and is mentioned in all the early herbals relating to food and medicine. It was grown in England in the gardens of monasteries and convents as early as the 9th-century and probably introduced to the country by the Romans. Water Mint was used as an early form of smelling salts and for the treatment of stomach upsets and earache. It was also used to freshen breath, as early as the middle ages. In the 16th-century it was strewn on the floor and as people walked on the leaves, the scent of mint was released into the air – a precursor of the modern air freshener. Water Mint can be used for a wide variety of contemporary recipes including cucumber and Water Mint soup, peas and lettuce with Water Mint, mint and apple sorbet and water-minty cider, as well as jellies, chutneys and tea. It is a particularly strong species of mint so be careful not to use too much.

## DID YOU KNOW?

Mint is thought to be named after the Minthe, a nymph loved by Pluto whose jealous wife turned her into a plant.

# Chicory
*Cichorium intybus*

**FLOWERING TIME** June–October

**HEIGHT** 1–1.5m

**WHEN TO FORAGE** June–October

**DESCRIPTION** Also known as 'wild succory', Chicory is a tall perennial herb with thick, fleshy roots. It bears clusters of sky-blue flowers that flower successively and are still in bloom in late autumn. They open with the sun in the morning and close around midday. It is the striking flowers that have given rise to a multitude of common names including 'blue dandelion', 'ragged sailors' and 'wild bachelor's buttons'. The stiff, grooved stems have branches rising at a steep angle. The stalked lower leaves may be toothed, or more deeply divided into triangular lobes. The upper leaves are stalkless.

**HABITAT** Chicory grows in fields, on roadsides and waste ground, especially on chalky soils. It can be found at the base of hills, along bridle paths and sunken ways along the Chilterns escarpment and along the Thames Path in Oxon.

**HOW TO USE** Chicory was under cultivation as early as the 16th-century and the leaves were often blanched for use in salads, forced in dark cellars or under flower pots. It was also grown as a forage crop for livestock. This plant is usually picked for its roots which can be dried, roasted and ground, and then either added to blends of coffee, or used on their own as a coffee substitute. Chicory seeds are sometimes sown with grass seed mixtures because the deep roots of the plant are useful in breaking up the soil. Young leaves are tasty in a salad, though slightly bitter, but older leaves should be cooked as a vegetable. Roger Phillips lists 'Chicory flower and cottage cheese salad' among his recipes in *Wild Food*. It can also be used with mixed greens and cooked with pancetta or bacon with olive oil and garlic, or served with anchovies. Supermarkets often stock several varieties of cultivated Chicory such as radicchio, with red leaves, sugarloaf, that looks like cos lettuce and Belgian endive with cream-coloured leaves.

**DID YOU KNOW?**

Country folk believed that water distilled from Chicory flowers was good for poor eyesight and for soothing sore eyes.

# Bilberry

*Vaccinium myrtillus*

**FLOWERING TIME** April–June

**HEIGHT** 20–50cm

**WHEN TO FORAGE** July–September

**DESCRIPTION** This bushy, deciduous shrub has wiry, green twigs and pointed, oval leaves that are bright green in summer, turning red in the autumn. The drooping pink or pinkish-green globular flowers are distinctive and appear in spring and early summer. In autumn, the fruits ripen into purplish-black berries with a blue bloom which are also known as 'whortle berries', 'black-hearts' and 'blueberries' (in the US). The Bilberry is similar in colour to the Sloe (see p. 41), but is slightly flattened on one side.

**HABITAT** The Bilberry grows on heaths and in open woods and thrives on high ground with acid and sandy soils. It is not common in our area, occurring mainly in Berkshire. The low-growing bushes are often hidden in among swathes of heather or under bracken.

**HOW TO USE** The mouth-watering berries are intense in flavour and can be eaten raw from the bush, though they can be a little acidic. Some people like to eat them in muesli or with fruit salad. When cooked they develop a delicious deep, juicy flavour and can be used in a number of recipes, especially puddings, pies, muffins, tarts, jellies, jams, and even wine. In Yorkshire, Bilberry pies, a mixture of Bilberries, sugar and lemon juice baked in a double crust, were the traditional fayre of 'funeral teas', served with thick cream. Locating a sizeable quantity of Bilberries is a challenge in itself, you may find just enough to savour in a bowl with clotted cream or add to a pancake or two. The taste is much more concentrated than that of their larger cousins, blueberries, grown in vast quantities in America.

**DID YOU KNOW?**

During the First World War Bilberries were gathered for use as a cloth dye, rather than as food.

# Blackberry or Bramble

*Rubus fruticosus*

**FLOWERING TIME** June–August

**HEIGHT** Up to 4m

**WHEN TO FORAGE** August–October

**DESCRIPTION** The Blackberry or Bramble is a fast-growing straggly plant that forms dense clumps. It has thick, reddish-green stems covered in thorns with prickly green leaves consisting of three or five large leaflets which have a silver-grey underside. In the autumn, the leaves turn into vibrant reds and remain until next year's leaves emerge. The flowers range from white to a deeper pink and attract a variety of pollinating insects such as bees, butterflies and hoverflies. At the end of summer hard green berries begin to ripen red, then deep purple-black.

**HABITAT** The Blackberry is so tough and resilient that it will grow anywhere, even up through a crack in the pavement. It can be found in woodlands, hedgerows, gardens, waste ground and roadside verges.

**HOW TO USE** The first berry at the end on the stalk is always the sweetest and is best eaten fresh from the bush. In the following weeks begin to gather the next ripest berries for use in pies, crumbles, fruit fools, jellies and jams. Blackberries can also be incorporated into autumn pudding or used in less conventional ways with meat, for instance, as a sweet-and-sour bramble sauce with pork. Blackberries have been eaten by humans since the Stone Age and just one or two generations ago 'going blackberrying' was a celebrated event in the family calendar across town and countryside. It is still a great seasonal activity and a few scratched and stained fingers is a small price to pay when you can return home with tubs of free, glossy berries. According to folklore, do not eat blackberries after Michaelmas Day (usually end September/beginning October), because that night the Devil goes by and spits on every bush. Happily, by this time the berries are usually too wet and mouldy to use.

## DID YOU KNOW?

There are thought to be 400 micro-species of Blackberry in Britain, each with a subtly different fruiting time, flavour and size.

# Fat Hen

*Chenopodium album*

**FLOWERING TIME** June–October

**HEIGHT** 20–150cm

**WHEN TO FORAGE** Any time

**DESCRIPTION** The name of this annual herb is derived from the German *Fette Henne*, as it was originally used in Germany for feeding poultry, to fatten hens. It is a member of the goosefoot family, which includes Good King Henry (see p. 35). The stems of Fat Hen are tough, stiff and branched. The leaves are thick, stalked and alternate, mealy whitish when young and roughly diamond-shaped, or as their name suggests, the shape of a goose's foot. The green flowering spikes have tiny clusters of flowers. The equally common and closely-related **Common Orache** *Atriplex patula* and **Spear-leaved Orache** *Atriplex hastata* have more triangular-shaped lower leaves and can also be used as a wild foods.

**HABITAT** Fat Hen is a very common plant and grows on any waste ground or cultivated land, particularly near buildings and on old manure heaps.

**HOW TO USE** Fat Hen's use as a food plant dates back to prehistoric times and remains of the plant have been found in Neolithic settlements across Britain. The seeds are high in fat and the leaves are abundant, providing a valuable source of food. The whole plant can be eaten raw, if the stems and leaves are young and tender. Otherwise, it is best cooked down in much the same way as spinach, so you'll need to gather a good quantity to make a serving. It is often served as an accompaniment to meat. Add a little water and a pinch of salt to a pan with chopped Fat Hen leaves, bring to the boil and cook for two to three minutes. Serve with butter and a sprinkling of nutmeg. The taste is similar to broccoli.

### DID YOU KNOW?

Fat Hen contains more iron and protein than either cabbage or spinach, and more vitamin B and calcium than raw cabbage.

34

# Good King Henry

*Chenopodium bonus-henricus*

**FLOWERING TIME** May–August

**HEIGHT** 40–80cm

**WHEN TO FORAGE** Late spring and summer

**DESCRIPTION** A handsome perennial plant, also known as 'mercury goosefoot'. It has triangular, spear-shaped leaves and tall greenish-yellow flowering tops that appear as spikes. Despite the English-sounding name, Good King Henry is a translation of the German *Guter Heinrich*, or 'Good Henry', an elfin figure from Saxon folklore, and was so-named to distinguish it from a poisonous plant known as 'Bad Henry', which it in no way resembles. Some believe that the name became 'Good King Henry' in Tudor England, in homage to Henry VIII.

**HABITAT** This plant grows wild throughout the three counties on waste ground, arable land, roadside verges, by hedges and near old buildings. It can be grown as a cottage garden herb as the leaves can be picked continuously, in a similar manner to everlasting spinach. It was grown in the gardens of monasteries and abbeys and can still be found within the ruins of Godstow Abbey near Wolvercote in north Oxford.

**HOW TO USE** Good King Henry was introduced as a vegetable from central Europe by the Romans, and was cultivated in medieval and Tudor times. As well as recommending the plant as a cure for several ailments, 17th-century herbalist, Culpeper preferred it to spinach, considering it superior in firmness and flavour. In the kitchen, it was a popular pot-herb usually cooked as a green vegetable and served with meat. Over the centuries the crop was valuable to poorer countryside workers and Scottish crofters often turned to the plant for a source of nourishment after field clearances. The young leaves can be used in salads and the young stems are similar in taste to asparagus, hence its other common name 'poor-man's asparagus'. Some cooks find the leaves rather bitter, so to temper the bitterness, you can soak the leaves in salted water for half an hour before discarding the water and cooking the leaves with a drizzle of oil.

### DID YOU KNOW?

Good King Henry is exceptionally rich in vitamin B, iron, calcium and protein.

# Juniper
*Juniperus communis*

**FLOWERING TIME** May–June; berries mainly January–June but appear all year

**HEIGHT** 1–3.5m

**WHEN TO FORAGE** September–October

**DESCRIPTION** Juniper is a spreading evergreen shrub with spikey blue-green needles in whorls of three. Each has a white band on the upper side. Small yellow flowers form at the base of the leaves in early summer. Berries are cone-like and green in the first year, ripening to blue-black berries in the second year.

**HABITAT** Juniper is one of the three conifers native to Britain and favours the warm, dry soils of the chalk downs. Though it is uncommon in the Downs and Chilterns, it thrives in the old chalk grassland on sites such as Aston Upthorpe Down near Blewbury in Oxon and at Oakley Hill and Chinnor Hill (Oxon) and Grangelands and Pulpit Hill near Princes Risborough (Bucks) in the Chilterns. It tends to grow in colonies which can be a noticeable landmark in the countryside.

**HOW TO USE** In the New Testament, Mary and Joseph, during their flight into Egypt, hid Jesus from Herod's soldiers in a thicket of Juniper. Since earliest times, it has been associated with refuge and miracles. In the middle ages, Juniper was believed to offer protection from witches, while its pungent smoke has been used for purifying the air, ward off disease and keep away evil. Together with beech wood, Juniper was also used to smoke and preserve hams. The berries created a brown dye and, used medicinally, was said to resist the plague and act as an antidote to poisons. Infusions of the berries were also believed to restore lost youth. Oil from aromatic Juniper berries is still used to flavour gin, giving it the characteristic smell and flavour, though berries are now imported when used by British distillers. Today's cooks sometimes use Juniper berries in a stuffing with pork chops or spare ribs and also game. A few crushed berries with some salt and garlic can also be used as a rub before roasting or grilling.

### DID YOU KNOW?
Juniper oil had an ancient reputation as an abortifacient and until the late 20th-century was used in pills and advertised as 'The Lady's Friend'.

# Crab Apple
*Malus sylvestris*

**FLOWERING TIME** April

**HEIGHT** Up to 10m

**WHEN TO FORAGE** August–September

**DESCRIPTION** The Crab Apple can be difficult to distinguish from apple trees that have hybridised and naturalised in woods and hedgerows, but the true wild species, also known as 'scrogs' or 'wildlings' is a small tree with some spines on the branches and twigs. The bark is reddish brown and the downy leaves are pointed oval in shape. The fragrant pinkish-white flowers open in spring from deep pink buds. In full blossom, a Crab Apple is usually buzzing with bees and other pollinating insects. The small, round fruits are yellowish-green and hang in bunches. In early autumn they become flushed with red, by which time the tree is often standing in a pool of fallen apples.

**HABITAT** The Crab Apple recolonised Britain after the Ice Age and is regarded as a native British tree. You can find it scattered throughout the countryside in the three counties, often in copses, thickets, oak woodland and in hedgerows. It is the most important ancestor of the cultivated apple of which there are now thousands of varieties, including Bramley's Seedling and Cox's Orange Pippin.

**HOW TO USE** Open, individual flowers of the Crab Apple can be crystallised with sugar and used to decorate cakes and ice cream. Since the fruits are small, hard and sour, Crab Apples are best used cooked, in wild fruit jellies and jams. They can also be roasted and served with meat, or added to warm ale and winter punches such as 'wassail', a traditional Christmas drink that features in the plays of William Shakespeare. Apple butter with dry cider, sugar and lemon rind is another good use. Wait for the apples to drop from the tree before using.

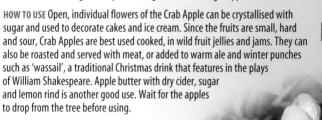

**DID YOU KNOW?**

The wood of Crab Apple is excellent both for carving and for burning.

# Blackthorn or Sloe

*Prunus spinosa*

**FLOWERING TIME** March–April

**HEIGHT** 1–4m

**WHEN TO FORAGE** Throughout autumn

**DESCRIPTION** More commonly known as Blackthorn, the Sloe is a branching, often crooked tree or tall shrub with dark, blackish-brown bark, twigs with long, sharp thorns and small, neat green oval leaves. It is the first tree to blossom in early spring, before the leaves appear, and has tight white buds that form in clusters and open into starry flowers with five petals and a ring of gold anthers. The fruits are miniature black plums, one of the wild ancestors of our many cultivated plums. As the fruits begin to ripen at the end of summer they are covered with a thick blue bloom, later turning purple, then a polished black.

**HABITAT** The Sloe grows in many hedgerows and can be found in abundance in the three counties, and gives its name to the village of Blackthorn on the Bucks/Oxon border. BBOWT nature reserves such as Bernwood Meadows, Rushbeds Wood, Upper Ray Meadows (Bucks), and Whitecross Green Wood (Oxon) are carefully managed for their Blackthorn, the larval foodplant of the scarce Brown Hairstreak and Black Hairstreak butterflies.

**HOW TO USE** Always pick your Sloes after the first frosts, when the skins have softened. You may prefer to wear gloves as the thorns can cause skin irritation. Sloes are most often used to make sloe gin, by adding sugar, gin and a few drops of almond oil. Left to mellow for a few months it should be ready in time for Christmas. Sloe also makes a good wine and, in the past, disreputable wine merchants would use it to adulterate port. Sloe leaves were also once dried and used as a substitute for tea. Sloe jelly and sloe and apple jelly cream are other appetising ways to enjoy these fruits.

**DID YOU KNOW?**

Sloe gin acquired its name of 'Mother's Ruin' over the centuries as the sloes were mixed with pennyroyal mint and valerian and used to induce abortion.

# Hazel

*Corylus avellana*

**FLOWERING TIME** January–March

**HEIGHT** 1.5–3.5m

**WHEN TO FORAGE** September–November

**DESCRIPTION** Hazel trees have shiny, smooth reddish-brown bark. The leaves are toothed and oval in shape, wider on one side with deep, wide-spaced veins. In winter the male flowers hang in yellow 'lambstail' catkins and the female flowers appear as tiny, spikey red buds. In autumn, the nuts develop in clusters of twos and threes, held in a frilly husk which turns brown and papery as the nuts ripen. The English name is derived from the Anglo-Saxon *haesel knut*, from 'haesel' meaning a hat or cap, referring to the green leafy cap encasing the nut.

**HABITAT** Hazel is common in woods and hedgerows throughout the three counties. It is a tree with many uses and to ensure a steady supply, bushes were traditionally coppiced at regular intervals to produce rods to weave coracles, baskets, panels and hurdles. Forked twigs of hazel were also used to great effect by water diviners.

**HOW TO USE** Hazel nuts should be gathered as soon as the husks start to dry early in the autumn. Odds are the local squirrel and mouse populations have been keeping a careful eye on them too, so you'll probably spot a scattering of nibbled nuts on the ground as early as July and August. Pigeons and pheasants also eat Hazel nuts. When picked fresh, the nuts are milky and sweet, best eaten dipped in a few grains of salt. As they ripen further, the nuts become crisper and drier. It is then that they can be finely chopped or grated and added to cakes and other desserts, such as hazelnut meringue and nougat.

## SIMILAR SPECIES

The Celts associated Hazel with fire and fertility and was thought by many to ward off evil.

# Sweet Chestnut

*Castanea sativa*

**FLOWERING TIME** June

**HEIGHT** Up to 30m

**WHEN TO FORAGE** October–November

**DESCRIPTION** The Sweet Chestnut is tall and narrow with many low branches which spread wider as the tree matures. The shiny green leaves are alternate, with saw-like teeth and parallel veins, turning a warm gold by autumn. In summer the tree bears long yellow catkins with a sickly sweet scent. The flowers develop into glossy brown nuts which are flat on one side and encased in spikey green cases, reminiscent of a hedgehog. **Caution: the Sweet Chestnut is not to be confused with the Horse-chestnut (conker) *Aesculus hippocastanum*, which is an inedible seed.**

**HABITAT** The Sweet Chestnut is fairly common and can be found in woods and parkland. There are impressive examples of old chestnuts in Windsor Great Park In Berkshire planted in the 18th-century.

**HOW TO USE** The most enjoyable way to eat Sweet Chestnuts is to roast them on an open fire on a chilly night. A rather risky method to tell whether they are cooked or not is to slit the skins of all but one nut and place them in the hot ash of a fire. When the uncut nut explodes, the others are ready to eat. Sitting well back from the fire is advisable to avoid flying fragments of hot chestnut. Sweet Chestnuts can be used in a wide range of savoury and sweet dishes, from the much-loved turkey stuffing as part of Christmas dinner, to chestnut sauce, and an accompaniment to Brussel sprouts or red cabbage. Candied chestnuts and chestnut soufflé pudding may appeal to those with a sweeter tooth.

**DID YOU KNOW?**

The Sweet Chestnut was thought to have been introduced by the Romans to provide a home-grown source of chestnut flour to make a hearty form of porridge for the legionnaires.

# Chanterelle

*Cantharellus cibarius*

STEM 3–8cm

CAP 2.5–7.5cm

WHEN TO FORAGE July–December

DESCRIPTION Chanterelles are bright golden yellow and funnel-shaped when developed. As the fungus grows larger it becomes flatter with a depression in the centre, until it finally looks like a little yellow umbrella. The flesh is said to smell of fresh apricots. Make sure that the gills (which are thick with a rounded edge) run down the stem (decurrent), this is a most important distinguishing factor. Two fairly common relations of Chanterelle are the edible Horn of Plenty (p. 69) and Winter Chanterelle (p. 71). **Caution: The False Chanterelle *Hygrophoropsis aurantiaca*, found with conifers, is not edible – it is more orange and smells more mushoomy. The poisonous Brown Rollrim *Paxillus involutus* is also funnel-shaped, but is ochre to pale brown and bruises chestnut brown when handled.**

HABITAT Look for Chanterelles in deciduous and conifer woods around Newbury in West Berkshire and from Windsor Great Park to the heath and plantation areas, south of Wokingham and Bracknell.

HOW TO USE Chanterelles are one of the most popular edible species of fungi, valued for their delicious flavour and firm texture. They are eaten extensively throughout Europe and sold in shops and markets. Chanterelles are particularly good when cooked with potatoes or eggs. Chanterelle omelette and poached egg with chanterelle are firm favourites. They also keep well for a few days and can be fried and stored and made into dishes such as Chanterelle sauce, cooked with garlic, shallots, stock, white wine and seasoning. To prepare the fungus the earthy stem should be trimmed off and the fungus washed well. As Chanterelles are quite tough they should be simmered for 5–10 minutes in milk, or water, before slicing and frying in butter for 10–15 minutes.

### DID YOU KNOW?

The name is derived from the French diminutive of the Greek *Kantharos*, a cup. There is also a white variety.

# Shaggy Inkcap or Lawyer's Wig

*Coprinus comatus*

**STEM** 8–25cm

**CAP** 5–15cm long

**WHEN TO FORAGE** Late summer–autumn

**DESCRIPTION** This tall, shaggy fungus is also known as Lawyer's Wig. At first, it has a white, almost egg-like cap covered with rough scales which lengthens into more of a candle, or folded umbrella shape. Eventually the cap dissolves away into a black inky mess, the black spores dripping down in a black liquid and staining the grass below. The stem is smooth and white. The gills are white at first then darken from pink to an inky black. It has a faint and pleasant smell. **Caution: The similar-looking but smooth-capped Common Inkcap *Coprinopsis atramentaria* has a chemical contained in it that when mixed with alcohol can make you sick, so do not drink when eating them.**

**HABITAT** The Shaggy Inkcap is common in fields, roadside verges, playing fields, parkland and lawns. It often pops up in clusters where the ground has been dug over.

**HOW TO USE** Collect this fungus for eating when it is young, when the cap is still in its candle-shape phase and the gills are pale. It has a lovely mild flavour and requires very little cooking as the flesh is delicate. Gently wipe the fungus with a damp cloth to prepare for cooking. 'Wig omelette', with four eggs, seasoning, butter and cooked peas makes a tasty dish, as well as Shaggy Inkcap in scrambled eggs, served on hot buttered toast. It can also be sliced and added to soups and stews, or baked in the oven with milk and seasoning.

### DID YOU KNOW?

The inedible **Snowy Inkcap *Coprinopsis nivea*** is similar in appearance but is much smaller and found in pastures on cow or horse dung.

# Beefsteak Fungus
## *Fistulina hepatica*

**SIZE** 20–40cm across

**WHEN TO FORAGE** August–October

**DESCRIPTION** Beefsteak Fungus or 'poor-man's beefsteak' is a red bracket fungus with a large, tongue-shaped fruiting body. The underside is covered with a series of tiny cream-coloured pores which closely resemble an ox tongue which has given rise to its other common name, the 'ox-tongue fungus'. When it is cut the flesh looks and feels like raw beef and oozes a reddish liquid. It grows mainly on oak trees fairly close to the ground. This species of fungus does not cause the timber of the host oak tree to weaken at first, but darkens the wood and produces an attractive pattern known as 'brown oak', which is highly valued in cabinet making and for other decorative uses. It is believed that Beefsteak Fungus is responsible for the hollowing of many oak trees.

**HABITAT** This species is fairly common in broad-leaved woodland throughout the three counties, and can often be found on oaks and Sweet Chestnut, on either living or dead wood.

**HOW TO USE** In the past, Beefsteak Fungus was often cooked and eaten as a substitute for meat. Be sure to gather a fresh fungus before it has become tough and woody. Wild Food expert, Roger Phillips rates 'butter-boiled beefsteak' as a 'five-star recipe' and one of his favourite fungi dishes. The Beefsteak Fungus is cleaned and finely sliced then placed in a frying pan with chopped onion and garlic. Barely covered in water, the fungus is cooked for 10 minutes. Pepper, salt, thyme and butter is then added and the cooking liquor is reduced to a thick sauce.

**DID YOU KNOW?**

Beefsteak Fungus is still sold at French markets today.

# Chicken-of-the-woods

*Laetiporus sulphureus*

**SIZE** 10–40cm across

**WHEN TO FORAGE** Spring–autumn

**DESCRIPTION** This bracket fungus is unmistakeable due to its size and vibrant colour. Thick and fleshy orange 'shelves' with sulphur yellow undersides form tiered clusters that overlap on the trunks of trees, giving rise to a host of other common names including 'sulphur shelf' and 'sulphur polypore'. Each bracket is fan-shaped with a rounded velvety edge. With age the bracket becomes tough and bitter and fades from yellow to white and is often dotted with beetle or slug and woodlouse holes.

**HABITAT** This parasitic fungus can be found throughout the three counties and grows on old broad-leaved trees, usually oaks, Sweet Chestnut or willows, at any time of year except winter.

**HOW TO USE** With a lemony, meaty taste Chicken-of-the-woods makes an interesting substitute for meat in almost any dish. Some people think it tastes like chicken; others describe the flavour as more akin to crab. It works well in curries, rice recipes, risottos, casseroles, or any egg dish. Be sparing with your cooking oil though, because the fungus can absorb oil like a sponge. The chef, wild food forager and campaigner, Hugh Fearnley-Whittingstall, is an avid enthusiast when it comes to cooking Chicken-of-the-woods. **Caution: A small percentage of people who try this fungus can experience an adverse reaction including nausea and swollen lips. So it is important to try just a little bit of the fungus the first time to see how it makes you feel.**

**DID YOU KNOW?**

As a 'polypore' Chicken-of-the-woods disperses its spores through small pores on the underside of the brackets.

# Parasol Mushroom

*Macrolepiota procera*

STEM 15–30cm

CAP 10–25cm

WHEN TO FORAGE July–November

DESCRIPTION These large, dramatic and handsome fungi appear during summer and autumn. At first they are egg-shaped with a double white ring between the cap and stem. As the fungus grows the ring becomes detached and loose on the stem, the cap opens and becomes bell-shaped and later like a wide parasol, or even completely flat. The caps are off-white and covered with large, brown shaggy scales. The pronounced white gills are free from the brown-flecked (snakeskin patterned) stem which is long, slender and bulbous at the base. **Caution: The similar Shaggy Parasol *Macrolepiota rhacodes* is also edible but has been known to cause stomach upsets and skin rashes in some people. It has a smooth whitish stem tinged pinkish-brown.**

HABITAT A fairly common fungus found singly or in groups growing in open spaces, by the edge of woods and roads, and in fields and pastures.

HOW TO USE These mushrooms are best picked young before the caps are fully open. Each cap should be wiped with a damp cloth before preparing for cooking. A single fungus should be enough for one person. The flesh is delicate and should be cooked very quickly. They can be fried as fritters in mixed herbs, stuffed with sage and onion or sausage meat, made into mushroom and potato scones, or cooked with pork, onions and walnuts.

**DID YOU KNOW?**

The seeds of fungi are called spores. One Parasol Mushroom cap measuring 10cm across can produce 16 billion spores.

# Giant Puffball

*Calvatia gigantea*

**SIZE** 10–30cm across

**WHEN TO FORAGE** July–November

**DESCRIPTION** The Giant Puffball can grow as large as a football and is spherical in shape. The skin is smooth, white and leathery to start, turning a muddy yellowish-green when old. The Giant Puffball appears to grow directly from the ground, with little or no stem. The naturalist Richard Mabey has aptly described these fungi as 'glinting like huge displaced eggs'. In his book, *Food for Free,* he continues, 'to come upon one of these suddenly is a memorable experience, only rivalled by the taste of the first mouthful'. The much smaller **Common Puffball** *Lycoperdon perlatum* (the size of an egg), a common woodland fungus, is also edible but a little mushy and without much flavour. It has a stem and a white rounded head covered in tiny conical spines when young, turning grey-brown when the spores are mature.

**HABITAT** This is an uncommon species and can be found almost anywhere, particularly in meadows and pastures and under hedges, where it is often found near patches of nettles.

**HOW TO USE** A prime specimen should be gathered young, when the flesh is still pure white. It is best stuffed with cooked rice, chopped herbs, butter and seasoning and baked in the oven for 20 minutes. A Giant Puffball should be enough to feed a large number of people. Alternatively, you can slice the fungus into steaks, fry, grill or bake in butter or bacon fat. Raw diced puffball can be added to salads with an oil and vinegar dressing. The fungus will also keep in the fridge for a few days.

**DID YOU KNOW?**

The name 'puffball' is a corruption of *Puk* or *Poukball*, anciently called Puck-fish. The Irish name is Pooks-foot, from the Saxon *'pulker-fish'*, a toadstool.

# Cep or Penny Bun

*Boletus edulis*

STEM 5–25cm

CAP 8–30cm across

WHEN TO FORAGE August–November

DESCRIPTION Also known as Porcini, this brownish fungus bears a striking resemblance to a glazed, round bun. A member of the Bolete family, it is distinguishable (like other members of this family) by its mass of spongy tubes instead of gills beneath the cap. The word *boletus* comes from the Greek word *bolus*, meaning a lump, or lump of clay. In America, Cep is also known as the 'king bolete'. It has a stout, bulbous, pale brown stem covered with a white net. The cap grows wider than the stem with age, becoming dry and smooth. The gills are white at first, then yellowish. There is no ring on the stem.

HABITAT Ceps are quite common between summer and autumn in broad-leaved and coniferous woodland, especially those with oak, beech, birch and pine. They favour warm woodland edges and grassy clearings. Many myths abound about the best time to hunt for Ceps, usually when there is a full moon. A few days after summer rain is usually when young, fresh fruit bodies are in their prime.

HOW TO USE The Cep is mild and nutty in taste and used extensively throughout Europe. To prepare, remove the stem and spoon away the pores, unless they are very young and firm. Ceps can be sliced and eaten raw or cooked. They can also be fried with garlic and parsley for 10 minutes, perhaps with potatoes, or grilled with fish. They are also delicious in risotto dishes and omelettes, and have enough flavour to make tasty sauces to accompany meat dishes. A recipe for ceps with paprika, in Jane Grigson's *Mushroom Feast,* recommends quickly frying the fungus with onion, garlic, tomatoes, butter and lemon juice, with sour cream added at the end. It is worth consulting the recipes of Roger Phillips in his *Wild Food* for many more ideas, including stuffed Ceps and Cep croutons.

**DID YOU KNOW?**

Ceps are one of the most famous of all edible fungus and six varieties could once be bought in London's Covent Garden.

# Horse Mushroom

*Agaricus arvensis*

**STEM** 15cm

**CAP** Up to 20cm across

**WHEN TO FORAGE** July–November

**DESCRIPTION** The Horse Mushroom is a large fungus, with a broad, white cap that sometimes grows to the size of a plate. It is very like the smaller **Field Mushroom** *Agaricus campestris*. With age the cap discolours yellow-brown when bruised. The gills are free from the stem and are greyer when young than Field Mushroom but still turn the characteristic dark brown of the mushroom family. The ring on the stem is double. These fungi often form fairy rings many metres across in permanent pastures. The flesh smells pleasantly of aniseed or almonds. **Caution: Horse Mushrooms bruise and turn straw yellow, but the flesh in the base of the stem does not yellow. Do not confuse it with the toxic lookalike, Yellow Stainer *Agaricus xanthodermus*, which has an unpleasant inky odour and whose cap turns bright yellow if scratched near the edge.**

**HABITAT** This fungus appears in manured meadows and beside bridle paths and other places where there is plenty of decaying organic matter. It also occurs near stables or fields where horses graze, which is how it got its common name. The specific epithet, *arvensis*, means 'of the field' or 'of meadows' – a reference to the habitat in which it is found.

**HOW TO USE** Horse Mushroom is a good edible species and can be used in any recipe that calls for large, cultivated mushrooms. Tempura is a good method for retaining its anise/almond character. It also works well in risottos and omelettes. If the mushrooms are domed-shaped they can be stuffed, or if they have flattened in shape, they can be grilled like steaks. You could also poach them in milk with thyme and seasoning and serve with hot toast. See Richard Mabey's *Food for Free*, for a recipe combining Horse Mushrooms with redcurrants.

**DID YOU KNOW?**

This species can be used for dyeing wool and paper and produces a yellow-tan colour.

# Hedgehog Fungus

*Hydnum repandum*

**STEM** 3–8cm

**CAP** Up to 15cm across

**WHEN TO FORAGE** August–November

**DESCRIPTION** A medium-sized fungus with a short, thick white stem. The cap is unevenly shaped with a wavy edge and covered with beige to pink skin, smooth and often cracked. Rather than gills, this species has distinctive spines on the underside of the cap that hang down like stalactites in unequal length. It is these spines, or tiny teeth, that lend the fungus its common name, the Hedgehog Fungus, also known as the 'wood hedgehog'.

**HABITAT** This fleshy fungus can be found in all kinds of damp woodland. They are fairly common and form small clumps and occasionally long lines. The smaller **Terracotta Hedgehog *Hydnum rufescens***, also edible, has a long stem and a pink-brown cap and can be found growing in spruce plantations.

**HOW TO USE** After you have picked the caps, clean out any dirt from the spines. Many foragers recommend removing the spines completely on older caps. The firm, crunchy flesh of Hedgehog Fungus is slightly spicy. It is good to eat after blanching for a few minutes before cooking, to remove a slight bitterness. Hedgehog Fungus can be poached in milk or stock for 15 minutes or lightly fried and served with toast. They can also be pickled or frozen for future use. Roger Phillips lists a couple of mouth-watering recipes including 'Flaming Hedgehogs' (chopped and fried with shallots, calvados cream, oil, butter, paprika and seasoning), and hedgehogs with cubed gammon steaks, cooked in stock or red wine.

### DID YOU KNOW?

The Hedgehog Fungus was first classified in 1753 by Carl Linnaeus, the Swedish scientist famous for his work in Taxonomy, the science of identifying, naming and classifying living things.

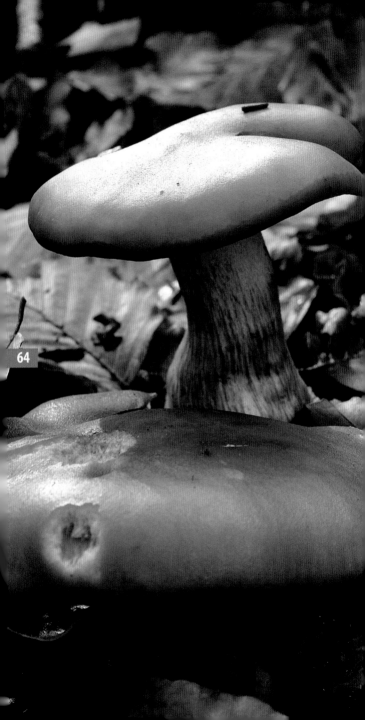

# Wood Blewit

*Lepista nuda*

**STEM** 5–10cm

**CAP** 15–25cm across

**WHEN TO FORAGE** September–December

**DESCRIPTION** When young the Wood Blewit is bluish or lilac all over, becoming whiter when old. The cap is sweet smelling and turns reddish brown or grey from the centre and the rim becomes wavy with age. The main distinctive feature of this fungus is its bluish-lilac gills. It has a stout stem which bulges more at the base but doesn't have a ring. It has a strong perfumed smell which does not fade with cooking. The closely related **Field Blewit *Lepista saeva***, another good edible fungus, has a clay-coloured cap and gills and a stem often streaked violet-blue (the name blewit is derived from 'blue-leg' after the bluish-violet tinge of their stems).

**HABITAT** This species grows in leaf litter and is common in mixed deciduous woodlands often on clay, particularly oak and beech, under hedgerows and even in garden compost heaps. Long after Chanterelles and most other popular edible fungi have disappeared Wood Blewits are still bountiful and, in some years, can be prolific. Head to the woodlands in the clay vales or to the clay-capped Chiltern woodlands in late autumn.

**HOW TO USE** **This fungus must be cooked and never eaten raw. It is advisable to try a small portion for the first time because it has been known to disagree with some people**. Wood Blewits are very good if sautéed and served with white meat such as pork and chicken; they are also fine with cheese, rice and pasta dishes. They can be stewed, used as an omelette filling, or poached in milk with chopped sage and served with potatoes. Roger Phillips uses them in a white wine and tarragon sauce to make 'blewit and chicken pie' with a short crust pastry.

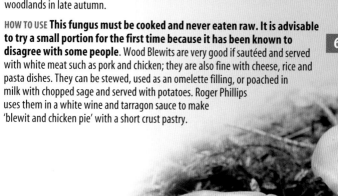

**DID YOU KNOW?**

Wood Blewits can be used to dye fabrics or paper a green grass colour when chopped up and boiled in water in an iron cooking pot.

# Oyster Mushroom
*Pleurotus ostreatus*

**SIZE** Up to 20cm across

**WHEN TO FORAGE** Late autumn–winter

**DESCRIPTION** The Oyster Mushroom can be variable in appearance, not only in colour, but also in form. Generally though, it is a fan-shaped bracket fungus, slate-grey or creamy-brown in colour with soft, white rubbery flesh. The white stem is off-centre and is short and thick. The gills are deep and white, and run down onto the short stem.

**HABITAT** This fungus can be found in clusters on the dead or dying branches and trunks of Beech and Ash trees. Some of the best sites to search for Oyster Mushrooms are in the Chiltern hills with their beech woods. These run from the Bedfordshire border in a south-westerly direction across the southern half of Buckinghamshire and Oxfordshire.

**HOW TO USE** Choose young specimens before they become tough. Check thoroughly for maggots and other creatures before preparing to cook. The Oyster Mushroom has a taste reminiscent of its namesake, as well as copying its shape, it is also similar in texture. Since it is a relatively mild flavour, it is best enjoyed with rich flavourings such as Madeira sauce or garlic and parsley. They can also be deep-fried, grilled, added to stews and casseroles, as well as dried.

67

**DID YOU KNOW?**
Oyster Mushrooms are one of the few wild species to be successfully cultivated and many supermarkets and delis now sell them.

# Horn of Plenty

*Craterellus cornucopioides*

**HEIGHT** 3–10cm

**CAP** 2–8cm across

**WHEN TO FORAGE** Summer–late autumn

**DESCRIPTION** Also known as the 'black trumpet' and rather alarmingly, the 'trumpet of death', this edible species has a deeply funnel-shaped cap with a flared, rolled-back mouth. The inner surfaces are dark brown to black, drying paler. The spore-bearing outer surface is ash grey, smooth then undulating. The stem is short and hollow, merging with the cap. The flesh is thin and leathery with no distinctive smell. There are no gills; the spores are white. A similar species, **Sinuous Chanterelle *Pseudocraterellus undulatus***, is also edible and looks like a paler, miniature version of the Horn of Plenty.

**HABITAT** The Horn of Plenty can be found in troops in the leaf litter of broadleaved woodland, especially beech or oak. To search for this species head to the beech woods of the Chiltern hills where they can be particularly abundant in some years. However, because of their dark colouring, they can be very difficult to spot as they hide among the leaf litter.

**HOW TO USE** Many fungi foragers consider the Horn of Plenty to have an unrivalled flavour. It is a favourite in restaurants where it is stuffed. It can be added to stews or soups as a flavouring or to improve the flavour of other mushroom dishes. It can be dried (over a radiator or in a warm oven with the door open) and then stored in airtight jars for future use. It is worth getting a copy of Roger Phillips' *Wild Food* for a number of recipes, including 'black trumpet stir fry' and 'black trumpet wrap' with warm mushrooms and humous. He also suggests a delicious pasta dish combining the trumpets with black olives, olive oil, garlic, fresh basil, pasta shells, seasoning and salami.

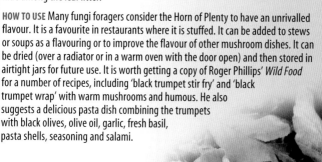

**DID YOU KNOW?**

In Greek mythology the Cornucopia (horn of plenty) had the power of providing unending supplies of nourishing food.

# Winter Chanterelle or Yellow Legs

*Cantharellus tubaeformis*

**STEM** Up to 8cm

**CAP** 3–7cm across

**WHEN TO FORAGE** Early autumn–winter

**DESCRIPTION** With their drab brown caps and flimsy flesh, Winter Chanterelles are not as attractive as the yolky-yellow Chanterelles that appear earlier in the year (see p. 47). Most obvious is the bright yellow/orange hollow stem which gives the alternative common name of Yellow Legs. The beige gills are also distinctive by being veined rather than deep grooved and run down the stem. The cap is convex with a depression in the centre when young, becoming funnel-shaped with irregular edges.

**HABITAT** This species is quite common but often overlooked. It grows in moss or on rotting wood in mixed woodland, especially beneath spruce and pine, though they are found under beech trees too. They can be found in vast numbers towards the end of the season. One of the best places to search for them is Bernwood Forest, near Oakley, on the Bucks/Oxon border.

**HOW TO USE** The earthy taste is stronger but less sweet than Chanterelles. Since they have a high water content, the fungi should be squeezed before cooking. Some cooks use the Winter Chanterelle in stocks, broths, consumés, soups and stuffing. They go especially well with rich, creamy sauces. They grow during pheasant shooting season and so they are often added to game casseroles, pies and stews. They do not dry very well.

71

### DID YOU KNOW?

In France Winter Chanterelles are known as 'Chanterelles' and Chanterelles are called 'Girolles'. To add to the confusion, some British supermarkets label Yellow Legs as 'Chanterelles' too.

# Species index